The Treasure Map

A Play

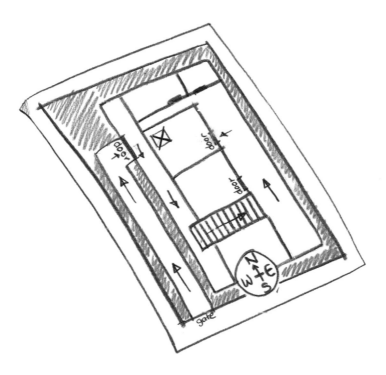

Maria Valdez
Illustrated by Karen Mounsey-Smith

The Characters

Narrator   Hannah   Mom

Dad   Grandpa

Narrator: Hannah and her mom and dad were at Grandpa's place. They were going to help him clean out his basement.

Grandpa: Thanks for coming over to help me. Let's start with these old books.

Hannah: That sounds like a good idea to me, Grandpa.

Dad: Here are some books I had when I was a kid.

Mom: Take a look, Hannah. There might be some books you'd like to read.

Narrator: On the bottom shelf, Hannah found a book called *Treasure Island*. She opened it. A piece of paper fell out.

Hannah: Hey, look at this! It's a map!

Dad: It's a treasure map. I made it
when I was about your age, Hannah.

Grandpa: It's a map of my house and garden.

Hannah: Can I hunt for the treasure?

Grandpa: Sure! Let's all look for it.

Narrator: Hannah looked at the map.

Hannah: Why does the map have letters in a circle?

Mom: That's called a compass rose. It shows you the directions— north, south, east, and west.

Grandpa: Can you see where the treasure hunt begins?

Hannah: The map shows that we have to start at the front gate.

Grandpa: Hey, this is exciting!
I didn't know there was treasure
hidden in my house!

Narrator: Everyone followed Hannah to the front gate.

Mom: Where does the first arrow point, Hannah?

Hannah: It points north. We need to go down this path beside the house.

Dad: Aha! I'm starting to remember.

Narrator: Hannah led the others down the path. Then she stopped and looked around.

Hannah: Look at these trees. They aren't shown on the map.

Grandpa: No, I planted them only a few years ago.

Mom: Where does the next arrow point, Hannah?

Hannah: Let's see. It points east, toward the back door.

Narrator: They all walked to the back door and went inside.

Hannah: Now the map shows some small lines. They must be steps. I think we have to go upstairs.

Grandpa: Yes, there are twelve lines on the map. And there are twelve steps!

Dad: I remember counting them when I made the map.

Narrator: Everyone followed Hannah up the stairs.

Grandpa: Do you think we're going the right way?

Hannah: Yes, the next arrow points down the hallway. We have to go to the second door.

Mom: I hope we're getting close to the treasure.

Narrator: Hannah led everyone to the second door. She opened it. Everyone walked into the room.

Hannah: Hey, Dad, was this your room when you were a kid?

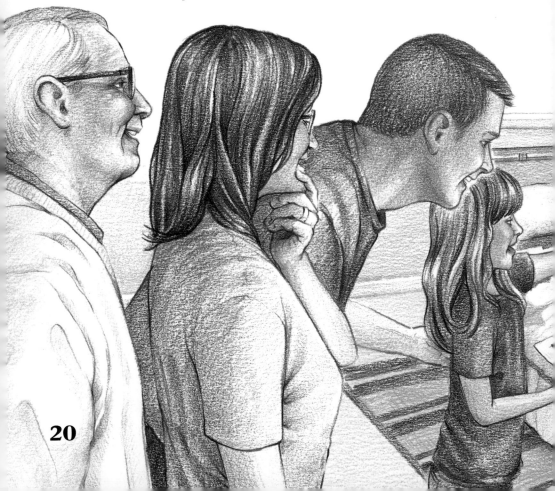

Dad: It sure was!

Hannah: The map shows an X
near that wall. Look!
There's an old trunk there.

Mom: I wonder what's inside it!

Narrator: Hannah opened the trunk. She found a box inside.

Hannah: This box has an X on it. This is the treasure!

Narrator: Hannah opened the box.

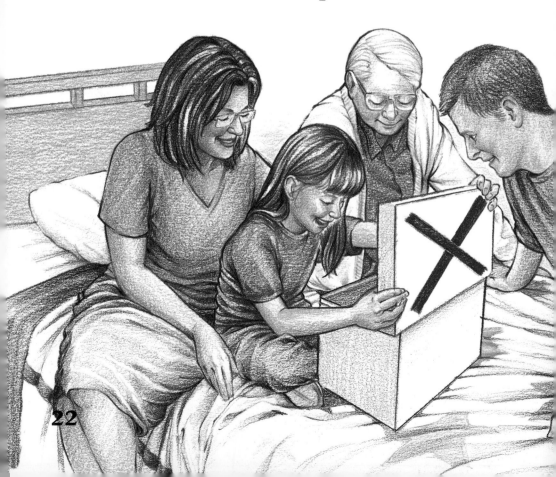

Hannah: It's full of puppets!

Grandpa: I remember those puppets.
Your dad and his friends used to put on
puppet shows for Grandma and me.

Hannah: Hey, Dad, let's put on a puppet show for Mom and Grandpa today!

Dad: Great idea! We'll do it right after we help Grandpa clean out the basement.